CHINESE LANTERNS FROM THE BLUE CHILD

ANTHONY MCNEILL

CHINESE LANTERNS FROM THE BLUE CHILD

PEEPAL TREE

First published in Great Britain in 1998
Peepal Tree Press
17 King's Avenue
Leeds LS6 1QS
England

ISBN 1 000715 18 X

CONTENTS

It is time, love, to break off that sombre rose,
shut up the stars and bury the ash in the earth;
and, in the rising of the light, wake with those who awoke
or go on in the dream, reaching the other shore of the
sea which has no other shore.

                                    – Pablo Neruda
                                    'The Water Song Ends'

POEMS

He brought light out of darkness, not out of lesser light; he can bring thy Summer out of Winter, though thou have no Spring; though in the ways of fortune, or understanding or conscience, thou have been benighted till now, wintered and frozen, clouded and eclipsed, damped and benumbed, smothered and stupefied till now, now God comes to thee, not as in the dawning of the day, not as in the bud of the spring, but as the sun at noon to illustrate all shadows, as the sheaves in harvest, to fill all penuries, all occasions invite his mercies, and all times are his seasons.

— John Donne

LA! ROSE SHE WAS LOVELY

I will tell you. Make a white mist in the mind; make that mist hang like cloth from the dress of a woman on prickles, on branches; make it rise from the earth, like the breath of the dead on resurrection morning, and I walking through it ... and ... I behold this woman, the loveliest thing I see on this earth, floating towards me, just like the moon, like the moon walking along her own road.

— from *Dream on Monkey Mountain*, Derek Walcott

La! Rose she was lovely
Remember her dark
Indianface

La! Rose she out-
shone
the sun

light and moonlight
She was a most luminous thing
She never came

home with me like
the rest
I guessed at her

under her printdress
One Sunday
I asked her in

to the river
A next one
I asked her

down to the sea
She never went swimming
with me

lovely Rose
She married another
La! Rose

she was lovely, the loveliest
thing Hist
Make a black mist

STILL GRASS

Some other has ceased to visit
ducks into the eye of the forest
skirrs over the floor of the sea
or spirals just-under the sky

too far-above-flesh to come back
too far underneath or secret
at any rate let go of me
Some other which startled to music
then hushed: the wind is too silent
Still grass underfoot made me stop

THE FA-LA FROM JENNY

Such pasts
Are not diminished distances, perspective
Vanishing points, but doors
Burst open suddenly by gusts
That seek to blow the heart out.

— Stephen Spender

But Jenny ex-/ miracle racer
skids off the last tarmac and stops
0 buckles her seatbelt and weeps
0 swallows ill capsules and chokes

on emissions   the Firestones lift
0 rockets The Sorrow head-on
0 petrified of the ignition
0 swivels the car keys at last

0 struck disremembers the G T 6
Triumph/I ruined another life
0 streaks back that other life
0 streaks back Brown's Town, Puert

-o Seco   0 streaks
back a green time before pain
0 streaks back her miracle racer
0 streaks through fleet Jenny eighteen or

nineteen/ 100 flat out in the wind
0 petrified of the ignition
0 Sorrows that fault us like engines,
then Jenny starts lovely in the green time

THE SUMMER CURSE
for Wayne Brown

1

A bomb ticks in the skull of the turtle.
Intractable cliffs
fissure to ash.

The God-/ genius
which piloted safely
snarls on a slick

Sargasso of muck.
The water rolls sluggish
under the weight.

Crude oil uncoils like a snake.

2

At sunrise
At moonset
The sky on the sea

submits a faint lantern
Underneath more coral declines.

3

Guns swivel & flash.
There is no cease-
fire: the explosion alarms

in Africa, Asia.
The continents reel
in their sons &

stand off.
By morning/ oblique
hurt is hatched from the coign.

4

And the turtle who risked the crossing
to spawn
skews on re-

crossing, flops far
up the beachhead & bakes. Her bones
flare   like maculate mother

-of-pearl.
The elements roil
to flower an answer.

Massed lemming, pre-set, self-destruct.

5

This is why the monk flings
A dirge on the mountain

why the girl takes the flame to her skin
why the trigger stays cooked

inside the assassin
why the struck Rastafari

dins a black note at the moon
why the Children miss poems

hush music, croak songs
why I croaked this one –

at last targetless.
A separate beam detonated The Curse.

THE CHAPEL OF DEATH/3

In the eye of the dark
a child lights

a yellowing candle
The flame

reawakens the room
[diminutive Dresden]

The memory hangs

I wonder who sings
sad
from the ruins

Somebody with wings

A WREATH FOR THE SUICIDE HEART

Somebody is hanging:
a logwood tree
laden with blossoms
in a deep wood.
The body stirs left
in the wind;
If the wind could send
its miracle breath
back to that person,
I tell you it would.
Love is Earth's mission,
despite the massed dead.
On the night of the hanging
The Autumn moon bled.

SISTER DOROTHY HART

for Mervyn. Dennis and Wayne

"In the Silent Air. ... Go back to Silence. Keep Silence. K.S.
K.S.... From Silence rewrite the message that is you. You are the
message I send to the Enemy. My Silence Message." The Naked
Astronauts were free in space ...

— William Burroughs

> Moon, it is a winter moon,
> A moth's wing netted in cloud.
> — Wayne Brown

The moon tonight
wears a sad colour.
I am thinking of Lisa,
met only once
ten days ago
very precisely
at the blue north.
She wades in the shallows,
lissom and tan.
She swims on her back.
When she settles, we talk.
My speech is tight
because I am nervous.
I am far too old
to be muted by shyness.
I tell her I saw
a film with her name, co-
starring an actress
who
shortly thereafter
hid her lush beauty in convents:
Dorothy Hart.
Anyway, as it went,

the actual Lisa, She
whom I sing,
said that my voice
triggered discomfort.
It made me stop sounding.
Softly now, wing

WILLIAM STEPS FORTH FROM THE TEMPLE OF STONE
THROUGH THE FATHER OF SHINING
For my true creator & family

I ride with the ghost
of myself
on Encavas

but the Father of Shining's
my seating companion
this time

and:
nothing can shift Him,
not even your gun

tracking my window,
not even the woman
who made me wish blood

for dumping red William
in a far time
and the summer moon rising;

So:

a liquid May morning
he kindled his work,

then his flesh;
So:
a lovely June evening,

still trained on it,
fell back from the tower,
dusting his feet,

twice then in one season
nearly became
xth guest in the icebox

ahead of us all
unless, like Elijah,
a chariot lifts us

by magic still somehow
wedded to breath
and wasn't he lucky?

unlike William "ailing"
29 years
"and all on account of *her*"

would seem a delusion
for
after all, junky,

for nearly two decades
you bored everyone
you could collar

to listen
by
passing the lyrics

from your stone temple
ad & ad &
ad nauseam

:

I love my poems above everything

WILLIAM CRIES UP TO HEAVEN FALLING THROUGH BIRDS

I

William kneels at a stone
of the Father of Shining
and prays to be shut,

to be borne up
by choiring cygnets
by miracle shifted

to fluently drift
great heights overarching
both space & time

beyond the glass ending
of Kubrick's *2,001*

:
Yes,
asks to be swept

to a high
sidereal locus
above any loft

where
sits on a cloud
the mystical Friend

and unending Font
waking the wrist
which issued his lyrics;

Cried thus
to the Lord God of Grace

:

"Take back my will,
Creator of Janus:
The gift of choice

In my case
leads only to error
and guilt-

shrouded sorrow;
I'm a needle
that jets out

a black snow:
Please destroy what survive
of my blasphemous verses."

II

The God remained silent
and glanced to the left.

The God remained latticed
and glanced to the right.

The God remained shuttered
and looked to the east.

The God remained cryptic
and looked to the west.

In the end one saw
nothing forthcoming

but slant
equivocal mirrors,

or else the unwanted
difficult tacit

religious directive
to go back down

to stash-&-M-16s,
a Lucifer-wedding

of Love
Death

as the ghost watched
;

for the junky, lost twin,
midnight envisioned:

a smashed vacuum
rooting in public

thru garbage cans,
the head

at last
emptied of

words
:

He did as his forbears, fell through the birds

1   It hasn't yet happened
Wing
on the fade

2   If you want not to be unlucky in love
Marry my poem
Instead

3   I can see beyond the most radiant future
The poem I'm writing's
A magic wren

4   I injured both badly and owned up years late
One couldn't forgive me
Thanks lovely other whose letters are flowers of faith

5   It's apparent my mother sees me as lost
I ascend in inches and topple in feet
My poem immune at the loft

6   When will you stop in the quince
Wren
From the winter-tree's silence

7   You appear in the middle of springtime as well
Hello Death
Angel

8   I'm writing this poem to you lovely Anne
For your paradigm-caring
Gone

9   It is time for us to lay down our guns
And break bread together
This in the interest of the doomed stars

10   God has no father
That's why
The sky's blue

AMERICAN HOOKER

American hooker
with Death through your body
Go home

You've snowed You've shamed
My brother My sister
Go home

Your cunt is a plant
for CIA missions
Go home

Your skin sets a germ
More invalid Lions
Go home

Your smile slits a husk
Blowing near oceans

Your soul runs a chalk
daughter of Sodom

Your heart mirrors desert
Ghost you tick on

Home
absent hooker
in the black dawn

whose angels are massing

Sing the stars down

27

THE BEAUTIFUL RAVENS

Father of Shining
I raise a wrecked wing

I spirit my song
through the Temple of Silence

Something ticks in me
like a bomb

set to ignite
any minute I think

to re-enter
the Garden of Twilight

and
when He complains

I remind Him of
the beautiful ravens

SOMEWHERE ON OUR JOURNEY
YOUR RIFLES STEPPED DOWN
for James Baldwin & V.S. Reid

Black woman I tell you you stop
my heart

riding Encavas
together; apart

for the curtain between us
visioned by Bwana

set by his wife
who

'offers and offers'
but

may as well rear
in the jungle.

for her
may as well ice

in the ghetto,
for him

may as well shot
through the nations,

for them
May as well drown

like
stone in the sewer

as-
sessed by such arctic

contempt
and that notwithstanding :

their rotten madonnas

their empty hosannas

their lethal dilemmas

the subtle despair
the Love caught

in the golden asylum

im-

maculate

One

:

Somewhere on our journey your rifles stepped down

THE KINGDOM OF MYTH/
A Fable in 32 Lines

Dog-heart's dis-
respect of the cold
Jungle or Tivoli don

left the youth dead —
from the waist down;
left the youth dread —

from the waist up;
Made him push night
with his right wrist

or else he was
a left-handed gun
like

the ghost of Paul Newman;
Made him cry to his woman
Go with Jah-blessings

my nature is gone:
Made him flex with his Bible

in search of a key

unlocking
Red City;
built skull on skull,

in the image of Hell;
Made him turn
and stay

to be
one with the fallen:
pious; touched; angry;

fatally slick; in
their crypts ruth
for the stretch.

His dust will inherit
His dust will inherit the kingdom of myth

THE SHORES OF TIME/I

Has it come to silence then,
spirit of song.

The words of the Graces,
muted by subtle prescriptions.

can't reach
from the floor of my heart.

Sometimes, flying
the fluctuant snows,

I once again come
on you bird.

But it is not the same
[came a wreath] anymore.

I swam & was happy;
There wasn't another shore

THE DOVE OF NIGHT/I

The dove of night
revisits in winter

There's a shift in the wind
A lovely chill enters

I cross to the top of the rise
with a lifetime of poems

They seem this evening nothing
at all in the sacred wind

NEAR WREN

He sings through wren
a near step beside us

the Father of Shining
whose star never dims

on his children
Both slant and sublime

Some of them prefer sorrow
and usher Him out

and ask in
the rain

inviting its mirrors
to flesh them again

CHINESE LANTERNS FROM THE BLUE CHILD

1.　　[21/1/93 - 28/1/93]
Tonight all the stars in the sky have gone out
And I'm sailing alone
In the ship of my body
Upon the night sea

2.　　[28/1/93]
I wander the world in search of my mother and father
I wander the moon in search of my brothers
I wander the stars in search of my sisters
Then they dawn on the valley
Lonely as God

3.　　[29/1/93]
Once long ago in a village in China
A boy cast word-lanterns
Before crossing the sea
He passed on the secret
of building
to me

4.　　[14/2/93]
I cannot remember who wrote the line
Though I sang in my chains like the sea.
How stupid of me
Summer night
Beyond the beauty of lyrics

PROSE POEMS

for Edward Baugh

How is it to be hopelessly in love?
Not bad compared to being born at all.
— Elliott Coleman

1. If God exists I'm in for a lot of trouble

2. Self-praise is a shining feature of cats

3. With a name like Enchanted Slipper how could the horse pull up

4. Life is too short," he said to his wife. They rhymed on something at last

5. Wild lily show me the way

6. *And* or & a major decision

7. Will the Gabor sisters ever age   please

8. "Why do you hurt me"   "I love you; that's why"

9. Word you are *wing* to the Father of Shining

10. Deep in my orchid book I miss my appointments

11. If I never saw an actual orchid, the word would suffice

12. The penis disfigures the male body. Necessary flaw

ANSWERS & CYGNETS/ 1-12

1.   Waiting in April the girl with wheat in her hair

2.   She said we were through, the summerbirds calling

3.   Something is dead between me and my mother. Only
     you loved back summer words,   summer colours

4.   What I fancied when young came true in my noon-time.
     Risky, said Goethe, to dream in the dawn

5.   Habits for some turn to addictions. The idylls they gave
     me were passing suns

6.   Money's success

7.   One bad father leads to a chain. Forgive me, my son,
     who also am victim

8.   Serenity comes from knowing my poetry's fate. This
     one's for the critics, who teach us our art

9.   Night fell of a sudden on me and no moon

10. I wouldn't have chosen another life. They say you ask to
     be born

11. Outlaws in great numbers have come to the arts

12. Evil accretes so forget it

1   For the psychopath liquor and drugs are accoutrements rather than props

2   I demand the right to assess the worth of my own life. Who else could open such involute dark

3   Blue is the shade of the most exquisite flower. The same as for ruined love

4   Christiana's lit violets are the gentlest blessings. But the pious detour them, walking to church and its contrary omens. Impaled on the eyes of the blind.

5   If the book you're reading's the worst in the world, give thanks anyway. The fret of misapplied words is deeply instructive.

6   I realised very early I had no gift for conducting a life. So I shifted my focus and sang a wreath

7   I arrive at the site of the graves, cast out by my fellows. Replaying the myth of the dolorous poet at odds with their rainbow eyes

8   The night of the golden fall still lifts in my rare recollections. I am subject to fleeting nostalgia, which I cast off. It is always now in the fields of light

9   For nearly two decades I've mirrored my madness in verse. And now that it's going I set the wraith.

10   Seven times I knocked at the gates with my tarnished submission. When they finally opened, I flew to the city of outlawed time

11   I have no right to mislike anybody. Each being a cell of
      the great God

12   God is both immaculate conscience and common sense.
      How strange to inhabit such contrary poles

WILLIAM RUTH'S JOURNAL OF THE ROSE MYTH
December 25, 1991 - June 26, 1995

1. Herb enforces the superego. William splits and judges his innocent myths

2. Unless you're utterly exploded, there's always something to be grateful for, Herzog reflected. I owe you one Bellow; our high classic humanist priest

3. The gulf between black and white seems almost a given. Some do the right thing. Make it wider even

4. The widow of a very accomplished poet and early friend "saluted" my not complaining about "an altered-to-nightmare life" in a recent letter. I thank her for this; but there are two things to be considered. One, I have to suffer romantic cliché and insist some verses were worth it. Two, it was always so in my secret heart

5. It seems commonplace to observe that for circa 200 years art has been a Janus; first for the artist, then his receiver. But I have to restate it, everywhere seeing the emptying fields

6. All morning I echo the song of the birds in the low branches. At noon I attempt to audit the sun. At twilight I shut down my verse like the fair hibiscus. Selvon was right. Of this I am certain. Everything that happens is words

7. 1 started with darkness, then fell back on light. But the sky has no place in a middle-aged psyche. It can't. We've seen it to death. Or — as truth is obversive — we haven't. Look up. It's still there. Near and round. A moon only possibly shining

8   My younger sister seems cut forever from her best – and, of course, oldest – friend, because the latter abused her. There are two sides, William says, to the matter. One is my sister, linking closely by right, love and She would scratch at this, who gave me sea-idylls

9   Life is a dream and we are its dreamers. I shift the glass truth from the dead. I'm flattered to have a hand in all this. Flowers. Mountains. The rainbow sun– All three imagined. And when we have gone, William says, the void come back will reflect everything

10   I'm falling in love with a grandiose person, who is also heartless and mean, he writes in his notebook. William Ruth in the mirror and lost. I myself won't have yet a third merciless lover. I myself will detour any woman that threatens to bring the night down. Rilke was wrong. The angels will stay, rewake without demons. For blessings are choric. I dreamed you before on the glass lake

11   Wordsworth was forebear to William's most grievous excess. Then the two argued. One certain of god as the sacred wood

12   It is strange Gregory Isaacs should mirror Lee Konitz. The latter's, however, is racial ice. Isaacs' chill goes deeper, a fatal attraction to death. Everything he sings resonates it. But he wouldn't say something as prolix as that. Dreads stepped forth, also for being laconic

13   Luck has no part in human affairs. We make even heaven with our own minds. This is the new parathinking. A form of self-consolation, given the omens. William improves it by dying again

14   A woman to whom I've written love poems for nearly a lifetime, failed to reply to my last four letters. Why don't you stop, says her silence, you know I can't love you that way. William, however, cannot give over her jet hair

15   The human condition wilts as it blooms. Like even stone, we enact fluctuation. We were born dying, but repress the fact till we're old and sick and the end comes back, this time in earnest

16   William and I both check for Keith Jarrett. His vast cosmic concerts were shaped on the run. Jazz piano in space, on Earth, underwater, even honky-tonk, depending on what the master crouched tracking. I'm proud to be brother – and racial – to him. Such music, God help me, knows everything

17   Those who write represent despair, and those who don't suffer in silence, Kierkegaard stated. This is how he divided the world. I alter his verdict to fit my work. Before the words knocked they had shifted. So I come to the steppe with the ash

18   William shuts in his room and thinks of the state of the planet. Like a mass of his fellows, he sees crossing signs of radical death and rebirth. With a halved psyche, he wonders which angel will win. I look through the doorway, equally split. The branches are silent. Then the last bird to vanish comes back, singing at darkness. Or else it does not. Either way the moon rises. It was always polar in wish

19   William reflects on one of his students. She writes very quickly and well. She's, in fact, by far the class's most talented member. He hopes her high gift won't pro-

gramme in nightmare. He prays she receive all the success he fleetingly knew. Walcott would say: "in another life". When the poet rehearsed winter lyrics. In the snows of wish

20. William has walked in the valley of shadow and felt the raven across him. It made horror visit, and psychic pain. It occasioned this listing to void. it invited the horsemen: Guilt and Remorse. I ask him to let up, re-issue the myth of the rocketing phoenix. He insists that he comes from the same ash

21. All day I worry the wounds I inflict on myself like additional shrapnel. The poet's first station. This statue of pain

22. One day soon I'll be not here forever. I hope you re-member the poet who sang of the girl waiting in April with midnight hair

23. If you hurt long enough, you transit to knowing. So the moon lowers its light. Fair it is was will be again night-grail on the fallen. Those angels invented by mist. William Ruth half-repeats it to wounded by omens the wish accretes

24. Sad songs attend William on his way home. He has fallen again. For months we stepped knit, avoiding and grow-ing. What made him come back to the City of Death was the fetal shift of this crossed composition. I allow it to rise; then instantly lower, knowing the ashes to come. But. 'Go forth, glass wing.' But. 'If demons dislodge me, it's angels I sing'

25. I love everyone in the abstract, but what comes back mostly is rock. A mete response really. The world, if not

actual, effects as concrete. In deeper recovery, I'll try for
its terms. If William wants to keep beating the wall, that
is his affair. I'll step down from dream and the mirrors of
summer

26   William thought such a love as he'd suffered for
       Catherine could never subside. Which it did as he turned
       from the shock. Here are the keys, said the Father of
       Planets. They will open a leveller life. One without her,
       or even your poems. In short, everything. At which he
       fell silent, all through the orchestras of spring

27.   William thinks on lost Catherine at the rose lake. A dove
       crosses over, lowering dark. In the sudden night I seek to
       console him. I offer a catholic line. There are other
       women. Everywhere. Look. He refers me out to the
       woman, asleep in the tower of myth

LANGUAGE-IN-MUSIC

*For my family: my mother, Lucy; my son, Patrice Dustin Pharoah
and my sisters Jeni and Carole*

[A] new form will always seem more or less an absence of any form at all, since it is unconsciously judged by reference to the consecrated forms.

— Alain Robbe-Grillet

THE GIRL IN GREEN
for Paulette

All women who leave me are you.
— from "Blues for Camus"

My sparrow you are not here,
Waiting like a fern, making a spiny shadow.
The sides of wet stones cannot console me,
Nor the moss, wound with the last light.
— Theodore Roethke

I

Perhaps I'd be better off sleeping than shaping this cry
        at three in the morning

Perhaps what I have *is* emphysema

Perhaps if I'm lucky I have a year left

Perhaps if I'd used competent tactics I wouldn't have lost
        the girl of my choice can't remember her name [she
        wore a green dress] tonight on safari

Perhaps if I hadn't been cautioned I'd have woken you up so
        early or late and said shyly: *Listen, Paulette, you'll
        think I'm mad, but I've got to speak to somebody...*

Perhaps I write mirrors

Perhaps there is sea in your hair

II

You say
you're a cat.

51

I find you more fawn,
quick and electric.

There are sonnets to make
upon your brown body:

It's grace-
ful and deft.

Paulette in the myth
you'll always be 20,

dancing
alone
to fast tracks

III

Listen, Paulette, I'm sick
of the pain

marries
the poet.

This late, in addition,
There's Lowell's night-sweat

IV

Why do I build you such verses

They'll fold the light interest you flashed

Who wants to hear failure & death above the work's subject

Yesterday evening you opted for music, versus my gifts

It stabbed when you said: "I'll check them out later"

When it came, I read to the stars

V

On the morning of signs we walked on the beach in the overcast
weather. I held a conch shell to your ear: "What does
that mean?" you questioned me, smiling. I wanted to
say, but wisely kept silent, afraid to be thought of as odd.
I will tell you now, since this song happened. What you
heard were the sighs of the drowned

VI

Paulette I'm tired
for not having slept
through the wound

It's probably four in the morning

I can hardly keep, as they say, my eyes open

It's crucial I shut   this prayer tonight

I give you the reason ::
Every day of my life seems the last

VII

Have I frightened you, sparrow
Sleep without care

VIII

I think you're ½-
lovely

That's nearly a rose

IX

I blend metaphors as a painter blends colours

X

The girl in green
is listing in bed
with the winner.

The loser twists sorrow instead

XI

I come to a hill,
holding
my hurt
like a satchel

At the crest there is frost

XII

All the women I've known in my life have been sisters
Can't remember her name

XIII

Paulette and the girl in green are the same